I0140547

HIGH

Matthew Lombardo

BROADWAY PLAY PUBLISHING INC
New York
www.broadwayplaypublishing.com
info@broadwayplaypublishing.com

HIGH

Cover Art by TheaterWorks, Hartford, Connecticut

First edition: May 2018
I S B N: 978-0-88145-760-5

Book design: Marie Donovan
Page make-up: Adobe InDesign
Typeface: Palatino

HIGH was originally produced by Leonard Soloway, Chase Mishkin, Terry Schnuck, Ann Cady Scott, Timothy J. Hampton, James & Catherine Berges, Craig D Schnuck, Barbara and Buddy Freitag, Lauren Class Schneider, David Mirvish, Gene Fisch, Stu Sternbach, David Fagin/Rosalind Resnick, Jacki Barlia Florin/ Michael A Alden and Lizabeth Zandel, The Shubert Organization (Philip J Smith, Chairman; Robert E Wankel, President) and The Repertory Theatre of St. Louis at The Booth Theatre in New York City on 19 April 2011. The cast and creative contributors were:

SISTER JAMISON CONNOLLY......................Kathleen Turner
FATHER MICHAEL DELPAPP...................... Stephen Kunken
CODY RANDALL...Evan Jonigkeit

Director.. Rob Ruggiero
Set design .... David Gallo
Lighting design .... John Lasiter
Costumes...Jess Goldstein
Sound design... Vincent Olivieri
Production stage manager .... Bess Marie Glorioso

CHARACTERS

SISTER JAMISON CONNOLLY, 55, a no-nonsense addiction counselor. Her tough exterior conceals an inner soul of guilt and shame. Chronically relapsing, she is hardly the picture of sobriety, and yet ironically she is the best at what she does.

FATHER MICHAEL DELPAPP, 43, a Catholic priest. Handsome and charming, he knows how to manipulate to get what he wants. He only allows people to see what he wants them to see. He's by the book yet a rule breaker, which is his lifelong conflict.

CODY RANDALL, 19, a drug addict in the final stages of his disease. His emaciated frame and blemished complexion were once that of the most beautiful boy. Angry, resentful and unforgiving, he is an unpredictable storm of emotions, and yet there is an innocence that lies within.

For what I do is not the good I want to do;
No, the evil I do not want to do—
But this I keep on doing.

Romans 7:19

For Christopher

ACT ONE

Prologue

(House lights fade as the sound of children's laughter can be heard. Lights up on SISTER JAMISON CONNOLLY.*)*

SISTER: When I was a girl I would read stories to my little sister before putting her to bed each night. My parents were both scholars. Dad was a professor at the local community college. And Mother taught academics to the underprivileged. Our middle class home was filled with books. Lining the walls. Stacked on coffee tables. Tossed about the floor—so that when company came they knew that this—*this*—was a well-read household.

I always let Teresa choose any story she wanted. Never coaxing her toward any particular direction or subject. Allowing her to decide freely what she wanted to hear. And night after night she would pick the very same book. It was the story of a boy who had the ability—*to fly*. And his travels would take him around the globe. Snaking through the California redwoods. Prancing with the African gazelle. Floating far up into a sea of constellations. And he would always pick one tiny star to take back with him so he would remember each and every journey.

Well, one night I finally asked the question: "Why, Teresa? Why do you love this book so much?" And she looked at me and said "Because that's where I want to be, Jamie—I need to be up there. I want to be—*High…*"

Scene 1

(FATHER MICHAEL DELPAPP *approaches* SISTER.)

FATHER: Why are you so resistant about this?

SISTER: Because I don't understand. Why me?

FATHER: You're the best counselor we have.

SISTER: Which is flattering but he's a much lower bottom case than we are used to treating.

FATHER: All the more reason to up your game.

SISTER: This kid doesn't meet our criteria.

FATHER: Our only purpose here at Saint Francis is to help those suffering from addiction.

SISTER: AND who believe in God AND who are Catholic.

FATHER: Faith and religion do not come as easily to some as others.

SISTER: Why not send him to a state-run facility?

FATHER: He would fall through the cracks and be right back on the street after his twenty-eight days.

SISTER: Who's to say that won't happen after he leaves here?

FATHER: Therein lies your challenge.

(SISTER *takes the folder from him, flips through papers.*)

SISTER: What about this fourteen year old? The Boy who died? Overdose?

FATHER: There was a puncture on the main vein of the forearm.

SISTER: And the drug?

FATHER: They call it a Speedball. I assume you know what that is.

SISTER: Could be any number of things. In most street cases, it's a mix of heroin, crack cocaine, methamphetamine. What else?

FATHER: It's all there in the report. *(He starts to leave.)*

SISTER: Wait. Back to the one who survived.

FATHER: Cody Randall.

SISTER: Was he arrested?

FATHER: No.

SISTER: Why's that?

FATHER: There was no crime committed.

SISTER: How do you know?

FATHER: Because although there was evidence of the Boy being sodomized—which appeared to be consensual—

SISTER: Still statutory rape.

FATHER: —there was *no* evidence of any semen present.

SISTER: Which fails to implicate Randall.

FATHER: Right.

SISTER: So what then? They just let him go?

FATHER: He was convicted on a minor possession count.

SISTER: Probably not his first.

FATHER: Then instructed by the State to enter a rehabilitation program.

SISTER: So no murder charges then.

FATHER: Never filed. No evidence. Besides. Cody claims he's innocent.

SISTER: And drug addicts *always* tell the truth.

FATHER: Those who wish to recover. Yes.

SISTER: Oh please. This kid's here for an oil change. A quick tune-up before he goes back out and starts playing in traffic again.

FATHER: Sister.

SISTER: Our benefactors aren't going to go for it. Our board of directors. What are they going to do when they find out we have taken in a homosexual, drug-dealing prostitute?

FATHER: The same thing Christ would do I imagine. Hate the sin. Love the sinner. Send more money.

SISTER: I don't remember that last being part of the catch-phrase.

FATHER: Vatican Two.

SISTER: Send him upstate. I have enough newcomers already. I can't take on another one right now.

(SISTER *attempts to hand* FATHER *back the folder.*)

FATHER: I don't recall *asking*.

SISTER: Pulling rank on me, Father?

FATHER: If memory serves you *do* owe me a favor.

(*Beat*)

SISTER: Why do you do that?

FATHER: Do what?

SISTER: Play the guilt card.

FATHER: I'm a Catholic priest. (*Attempting charm*) Come on. Do this for your favorite reverend?

SISTER: Father Anthony is my favorite.

FATHER: Then do this for your second favorite reverend.

SISTER: That would be Father John.

FATHER: Then do this for—

SISTER: You're not even in my top ten.

FATHER: *(Genuinely)* Look. This kid needs our help. So alright. He doesn't fit the cozy little picture of those who usually come in here. The devoted Christian husband who has too many cocktails before coming home from work. Or the straight A student who takes speed to help her studies so she can get into an Ivy League college. And yes. This one *is* different. But he shouldn't be punished for being worse off than the others. Sister. He has no one.

SISTER: Not our problem.

FATHER: But it is our duty. That's what we do here.

SISTER: He's going to lower my track record.

FATHER: Not a chance. And who knows? You might even learn something from this one.

Scene 2

SISTER: I was often teased in grade school for not being a very good student. Unlike Teresa, who always made academics a priority. That and torturing the swarm of boys who had insatiable crushes on her. With her long auburn hair and green eyes. That soft, freckled complexion. The way she would laugh when she tossed her head back. Giggled rather. *(Imitates her)* Ohh. Teresa had it all. Brains and beauty. Me? I didn't really have much of either. Well. Not that I would admit to anyway. No. I—I settled most of the time. At school. With friends. With boys that I would let— *(Her voice trails off.)* There was one in particular. A boy. He was all lanky and tattooed. A "redneck" for want of a better word. His job was to spray disinfectant in the shoes over at the local bowling alley. And ohh, I used to go there every day after school my senior year just to gawk at him for hours. And I knew. That he was no good. That he had a record. That he had just been released from prison for attempted armed robbery— which admittedly intrigued me all the more. That ever attractive degree of unspoken danger I had been thirsting for. As long as I could remember. You see, fear of the unknown can provide the ultimate rush for some. For most I imagine. And as much as we try to suppress it? That type of longing never quite goes away.

Scene 3

(CODY RANDALL *approaches* SISTER.)

CODY: You Sister Jamison?

SISTER: You're late.

CODY: Yeah. But.

SISTER: We had an appointment this morning. It is now afternoon.

CODY: Yeah. But.

SISTER: Yeah but nothing! And just for the sake of clarity: "Yeah" is not a word and "but" most often precedes an excuse which I am notorious for never accepting.

CODY: I overslept.

SISTER: Tough shit.

(CODY *looks at* SISTER, *surprised.*)

SISTER: Those two words are cousins to "yeah-but".

CODY: Look. I.

SISTER: Suppose you were the one on time and I showed up five hours late?

CODY: I'd get over it.

SISTER: You'd also be in some God-forsaken hell-hole pushing a needle half-way up your vein—or from what you are probably covering up, any vein you haven't collapsed yet in an effort to blame me for your current situation.

(CODY *is about to speak but* SISTER *interrupts him.*)

SISTER: You see how detrimental excuses can be? Do you not smell the evil in explanation? I never explain myself to anyone because I never have to be excused for anything I do. And may I suggest, Mr Yeah-But, that if you hope to carve out any sort of a life for yourself, you will start by taking on as much responsibility as you can handle—which given your current state, I'm assuming will be minimal.

CODY: Alright. Chill. I'll get here on time from now on. Sorry.

SISTER: And I don't accept apologies for situations that can be prevented and yours certainly lacked sincerity.

CODY: Then I'm not sorry.

SISTER: Sit down.

CODY: No.

SISTER: You'll be more comfortable.

CODY: Yeah? Well, you don't know me.

SISTER: (*Amused*) Don't I? (*Beat*) They had you in lockdown?

CODY: Yeah.

(SISTER *gives* CODY *a look.*)

CODY: Yes.

SISTER: How long?

CODY: I dunno. I guess I was in that nuthouse for like two weeks.

SISTER: Psych ward?

CODY: Yes.

SISTER: You must have done quite a number on yourself for them to keep you there so long.

CODY: I tried.

SISTER: And how do you feel now? Better?

CODY: Better than what?

SISTER: Better than before.

CODY: I don't remember before.

SISTER: Still having suicidal thoughts?

CODY: Why? You got any to spare?

(SISTER *looks back into the folder, jots down a note.*)

CODY: Hey. What are you writing?

SISTER: That you are a freak.

CODY: Come on. I'm serious.

SISTER: So am I. *(She writes)* "Cody Randall is a freak!" *(She shows him the paper.)* They have you in residence now?

CODY: Huh?

SISTER: You're living *here*. With the others?

CODY: Uhh-huh.

SISTER: Beats living on the streets.

CODY: Yeah. Like you'd really know anything about that.

SISTER: Ohh. Little-boy. Little-boy. So unique. Like no one knows what it's like to be you. As if you're the first person who's ever come through that door with a drug problem. Let me tell you something. You're not. You're garden variety. And the sooner you get that? The sooner you're going to get better.

Oh, and in reference to your little quip before? I *was* homeless. Three and a half years I was out there. Hated every waking minute of it. Well. Any minute that I could remember. Booze has a way of making things more bearable when you don't have a home. Or if you're really lucky? It can wipe a memory completely away.

CODY: I thought you were like a nun or somethin'.

SISTER: I am. Wasn't then. No. Then? I was. Well. Let's just say I was—something else. That's perhaps why Father Michael thinks I can help you.

CODY: Look. Lady. I don't mean to piss on all this recovery shit you got going on here. But ain't you supposed to be. I mean isn't all this just kind of. I dunno. I mean. I dunno. You know what I'm saying?

SISTER: Your postcards must be a riot to read.

CODY: I mean like you and me? You being a girl and shit. Shouldn't I be talking to another dude or somethin'?

SISTER: Oh. Well. That. Yes. That is the norm for this type of procedure. But that rule mostly is suggested so the subject doesn't act upon any romantic or sexual feelings he/she may develop for his/her counselor. That happens quite often. Sinner falls in love with Savior. We call that the Mary Magdalene complex. But considering I'm a nun sworn to celibacy and you're an active homosexual? I really don't see us fucking anytime soon.

Yeah. I know. One of my character defects. I curse. A lot. You'll get used to it. Or you won't. I don't give a shit. And it's not like I haven't tried to give it up.

I have. But attempting to get sober and quit using profanities was far too much for me to accomplish in one lifetime. So my then-sponsor, decided it was far better to concentrate on the defect that was killing me rather than the one that was impolite cocktail conversation. But I'm much better now: I don't swear half as much as I fucking used to.

CODY: You drank?

SISTER: Jack Daniels girl. When I could get it. When I couldn't? Rubbing alcohol. And when I was completely broke? I would hang out in the baking goods aisle of the A and P and chug bottles of vanilla extract. You can get quite a buzz from that shit.

CODY: *(Smirks)* That's fucked up.

SISTER: What about you? You drink?

CODY: Naah.

SISTER: Just the hard stuff.

CODY: Right on.

SISTER: Alright. Suppose we list everything.

CODY: Huh?

SISTER: All the narcotics you've taken. For reference purposes.

CODY: That's lame. I don't want to do that.

SISTER: You really don't seem to grasp the dynamic here, do you? See. When I ask you do something? You do it. I'm not looking for a big song and dance. I really don't care what you want. Because when left to your own devices? Your best thinking got you here. Get me?

(CODY remains silent.)

SISTER: I'm sorry. Am I talking to the fucking wall? I expect a response. A simple "Yes, Sister" will suffice.

CODY: *(Begrudgingly)* Yes. Sister.

SISTER: Thank you. Now. I would like to know all the drugs you have used.

CODY: Umm. Alright. I've smoked pot.

SISTER: Who hasn't?

CODY: Cocaine.

SISTER: Child's play.

CODY: Shrooms. Acid.

SISTER: I did all that shit in the seventies.

CODY: Rufies. Angel dust. Crack. Special K. Crank. Mesc. Oxy.

SISTER: Slow down.

CODY: Addys. Perks. X. Klonnies. Hash. Reds—

SISTER: Whoa! Maybe we should list the drugs you *haven't* tried.

CODY: Yeah Sister, there ain't a drug out there I *haven't* tried.

SISTER: Then good for you. Really. That's good. You've done it all. I applaud that.

CODY: You really don't seem like a nun.

SISTER: Why? Cause I'm not in the standard garb?

CODY: What do you mean?

SISTER: You know. The headpiece. The veil. The rosary. No. All that's changed now. At least with me anyway. Today it comes down to two things. This pin of the Crucified Christ acknowledges my commitment to serving others. And this ring on my left hand symbolizes my commitment to serving God.
So yes, I am a nun. And yes, I am a recovering alcoholic. And yes, Cody Randall—I can help you.

(CODY *turns away.*)

SISTER: Tell me about the Boy.

CODY: *(Defensive)* I told everyone already.

SISTER: Not me.

CODY: They said I wouldn't have to talk about this no more.

SISTER: Were you involved with him?

CODY: Kind of.

SISTER: How long?

CODY: I dunno.

SISTER: Ballpark.

CODY: I dunno! Six months maybe.

SISTER: And your relationship?

CODY: What do you mean?

SISTER: Sex.

CODY: Yeah. So what?

SISTER: He was fourteen.

CODY: He told me he was older.

SISTER: And you believed him?

CODY: What the fuck difference does it make?

SISTER: Doing drugs with a fourteen year old?

CODY: He was using way before he met me.

SISTER: Then of course. That's alright then. That excuses you.

CODY: Look lady: I don't want to be here anymore than you want me to be.

SISTER: Then leave.

CODY: I can't.

SISTER: Why not?

CODY: Cause they'll put me away.

SISTER: So you're just using us.

CODY: Ain't you got that backwards?

SISTER: What could I possibly gain from the likes of you?

CODY: You people. You make yourselves feel better by trying to help guys like me. With all your smart talk and your recovery bullshit. Well, I'm telling you right now lady. It ain't gonna work! Cause I want to get clean just about as much as you want to get High.

Scene 4

(FATHER *approaches* SISTER *with a letter in hand.*)

FATHER: What is this?

SISTER: Looks like a piece of paper.

FATHER: I know it's a piece of paper, Sister.

SISTER: Then why did you ask?

FATHER: What is *written* on this piece of paper?

(FATHER *shows* SISTER *the letter.*)

SISTER: A change of schedule request.

FATHER: Why did you send this to the Archbishop instead of me? You know I'm in charge of any alterations to our program here.

SISTER: Would you have granted it?

FATHER: No.

SISTER: That's why I sent it to the Archbishop.

FATHER: Well for your information he has sent it back to me. And I have denied it.

SISTER: Oh, for Christ's sake!

FATHER: And taking our Lord's name in vain will hardly help your cause. Let alone your afterlife.

SISTER: This schedule you have us on is inhumane.

FATHER: Morning meetings are critical in recovery.

SISTER: For whom?? I'm half asleep. The patients can't focus.

FATHER: I would think you would embrace the morning, Sister. Didn't you get up this early at the convent?

SISTER: No. And we didn't make bread and cheese for the townspeople.

FATHER: God frowns on sarcasm.

SISTER: I'm sure He's thrilled with you making us pray at sunrise.

FATHER: And what did you pray for *this* morning?

SISTER: Later daylight.

(FATHER *is humored.*)

SISTER: What?

FATHER: Why this?

SISTER: What do you mean?

FATHER: Of all the things you could have become. Why did you become a nun?

SISTER: Contrary to what you may think, I didn't have a lot of options.

FATHER: You could have gotten married.

SISTER: That would have been problematic.

FATHER: Why's that?

SISTER: I think men are assholes.

FATHER: Present company excluded.

SISTER: No. Not really.

FATHER: Come on. Seriously.

SISTER: What?

FATHER: Why did you become a nun?

(SISTER *thinks for a moment, then cryptically:*)

SISTER: To find forgiveness. To seek redemption. I mean, isn't that what we all really want? Why people come to us?

FATHER: And how *are* the newcomers faring?

SISTER: Ehh. Batshit crazy. Willful. Defiant. And reek of cigarettes. Since when did we start letting them smoke?

FATHER: Since that study came out last month about replacing one's addiction.

SISTER: That's crap.

FATHER: I assumed you would subscribe to that philosophy.

SISTER: That we encourage our patients to substitute one addiction for another? No way.

FATHER: Come on. What would you rather? Have a patient smoke crack or cigarettes?

SISTER: Oh please—

FATHER: Drink a bottle of vodka or eat an entire chocolate cake?

SISTER: —that's hardly—

FATHER: Too many pills or too much sex?

SISTER: —a justifiable comparison.

FATHER: It's always going to be something. We all suffer from some form of addiction.

SISTER: And yours being? (*Pause*) Father, are you holding something back from me?

FATHER: About?

SISTER: Cody Randall.

FATHER: How so?

SISTER: It just seems peculiar.

FATHER: Oh?

SISTER: We've never had anyone like him here.

FATHER: Sister, how long have you known me?

SISTER: Longer than I care to admit.

FATHER: And in that time, have I ever given you cause to question my moral principles, my values.

SISTER: Not even once. No.

FATHER: Then why do so now?

SISTER: Because it doesn't make sense.

FATHER: You're spinning over nothing.

SISTER: I mean, why insist on bringing this kid here.

FATHER: Sister.

SISTER: Unless of course you had a motive of some kind.

FATHER: Just leave it alone.

SISTER: Are you fucking him?

FATHER: No.

SISTER: Then why is he here?

FATHER: Because Cody Randall is my sister's son.

(Beat)

SISTER: Why the hell didn't you tell me this before?

FATHER: You wouldn't have agreed to help him.

SISTER: I *didn't* agree if you remember.

FATHER: Look. I'm sorry. But the only thing that matters now is that Cody is safe.

SISTER: No-no. This changes everything. I can't disclose any information to you now.

FATHER: All client files are subject to my review.

SISTER: Not if you're a family member. It would violate his patient rights.

FATHER: Sister, that isn't how —

SISTER: You want me to help your nephew? Then we do things by the book. And that means protecting this patient's confidentiality.

FATHER: *(Reluctantly)* Alright.

SISTER: And you can't tell Cody I know he's your nephew.

FATHER: Why not?

SISTER: If he knows anything more then it becomes all about you and your relationship to him, or your relationship to his mother, or your relationship to me. No. It has to be about me and him for now.

FATHER: Fine.

SISTER: Oh, and Father? Don't expect too much.

FATHER: That's where you're wrong. Cody *is* going to get better.

SISTER: How do you know that?

FATHER: Because he can't get any worse. And it's your job to see that he doesn't.

SISTER: I can't control that. If Cody doesn't want to be saved, there is no salvation.

FATHER: That's not for you to predetermine. See, I believe in the miracle of healing.

SISTER: So do I. But only to someone who asks for the miracle. Who believes it is possible.

FATHER: That's a rather limiting concept of faith.

SISTER: You're missing *(the point)*—

FATHER: God grants miracles to those He chooses. Asked for or not. And what He has given us now is an opportunity. So rather than moan and complain about this supposed waste of your time or what miracle God would or would not grant. Stop thinking about yourself. Address your own addiction—to Pride. Allow God to work and speak through you. For then and only then—can the miracle occur.

Scene 5

(CODY *approaches.*)

CODY: I'm here.

SISTER: And late. Again.

CODY: We said three o'clock on Tuesday. It's three o'clock.

SISTER: Today is Wednesday.

CODY: Fuck. You're not gonna rat me out, are you?

SISTER: We're under strict guidelines from the State. I not only have to report your progress but any absences that may occur.

CODY: *(Flirting)* Oh come on, Sister. Please?

SISTER: Yeah. Whatever this is you're working right now which I'm sure is quite effective on sixty year old men with low self-esteem and hundred dollar bills in their pocket—it's lost on me. Really. I don't find you the least bit attractive or charming. In fact, when I look into your angry, bitter and resistant face—all I see is a kid who's scared shitless. Now take a seat.

CODY: Look lady. This is stupid! Why do we gotta keep seeing each other if I don't want to get clean?!

SISTER: Okay. First of all. You call me "lady" one more time and I will make you cry. Secondly, did I or did I not make it abundantly clear in our first meeting that I do not care what you want? So sit your candy ass down and let's get to work.

CODY: But—

SISTER: *(Overlapping)* And shut the fuck up.

(CODY reluctantly takes a seat.)

CODY: You creep me out when you do that.

SISTER: What?

CODY: Swear. It's creepy.

SISTER: Too bad.

CODY: You're a nun. Nuns don't swear.

SISTER: And nineteen year old boys don't try to kill themselves. *(Beat)* Tell you what. I will attempt to curb my tongue if you will give this a chance. Deal?

CODY: I don't trust you.

SISTER: No?

CODY: I don't even like you.

SISTER: And you are such a prize. *(Beat)* Now. Tell me about your family.

(CODY looks at SISTER then looks away.)

SISTER: Ohh. So we're gonna play *that* game, are we? Well, I've got a better one for you. It's called Either-You-Start-Talking-Right-Now-Or-I-Turn-Your-Scrawny-Ass-Over-To-The-State.

(No response. SISTER starts for the door.)

CODY: Alright. I'm talkin'. I'm talkin'.

SISTER: Good. Now. Let's start with your father.

CODY: I don't know.

SISTER: You don't know what? That you have a father?

CODY: No. I know I got one.

SISTER: What then?

CODY: Never met him. I don't know who he is.

SISTER: And your mother? Do you know who *she* is?

CODY: Yeah. She's a whore.

SISTER: Now we're getting somewhere. A whore for what? Money? Drugs? Sport?

CODY: All of the above.

SISTER: I'm guessing she was an addict as well?

CODY: Smack.

SISTER: Heroin?

CODY: Yeah.

SISTER: Where is she now?

CODY: She O Dd a few years ago.

SISTER: I'm sorry.

CODY: I'm not.

SISTER: So your mother was a prostitute.

CODY: Mmm-hmm.

SISTER: How did she hook up? With men I mean.

(No answer)

SISTER: Talk to me.

CODY: I waited outside bars and strip clubs. Bring guys back to our trailer. That's how I made extra money.

SISTER: How old were you?

CODY: Seven. Eight maybe.

SISTER: Brothers? Sisters?

CODY: Naah. She didn't want any more kids after me. She would, umm, go see this doctor guy all the time.

SISTER: To have abortions.

CODY: Yeah. So she didn't make the same mistake.

SISTER: Is that what she told you? That you were a mistake?

(No response)

SISTER: Go on.

CODY: Go on what?

SISTER: When was the first time you tried drugs?

CODY: I dunno. I think I was like ten.

SISTER: How did it happen?

CODY: One of Mom's regulars used to give me half a joint to smoke. It made me feel good. So I did it.

SISTER: And your mother knew?

CODY: That bitch was too tweaked out most of the time to know much of anything. She'd be all shaky and shit. Would end up making a mess of herself every time she tried to find a vein.

SISTER: And that upset you?

CODY: Kind of. I mean, no one wants to see their Mom— *(He trails off.)*

SISTER: So what did you do?

CODY: I started helping her. Ya know? So she wouldn't hurt herself no more.

SISTER: Meaning?

CODY: She taught me how to do it.

SISTER: Inject her with heroin?

CODY: Yeah. I was really good at it too. I could hit almost every time. And it was tricky with Mom, ya know? Cause her veins were so shot? I'd always have to pull out a little to see if blood would spill up in the syringe—and once that'd happen I'd shoot it fast and BAM! Her eyes would go back in her head. And she'd get that cough. Ya know. That's how you knew you hit it hard. Her speech would get all slurred and stuff. And then her body would just— (*His mood changes, stopping mid-sentence*)

SISTER: When you saw that look on your mother's face? The one you just described? How did that make you feel?

CODY: At first? It scared the hell outta me. I mean, it was kinda like she died but was still breathing. Weird shit. But then? I dunno. I was. I thought. I mean. If something could make her feel that good? Maybe it could do the same for me.

SISTER: You were that unhappy.

CODY: I hated my fucking life. And I sure as hell hated her. So.

SISTER: So that's when you started using.

CODY: Yeah.

SISTER: You inject yourself?

CODY: Mmm-hmm.

SISTER: Were you alone?

CODY: No.

SISTER: Who was with you?

CODY: That guy.

SISTER: What guy?

CODY: The one who used to give me them half-smoked joints? I told him what I was going to do. So he hung around. Ya know. Case anything bad happened.

SISTER: Where was your mother during all this?

CODY: Probably passed out somewhere.

SISTER: Go on.

CODY: *(Clamming up)* That's it.

SISTER: Don't do that, Cody.

CODY: Can I go back to my room now?

SISTER: Tell me what happened.

CODY: What's to tell? I shot up and got High.

SISTER: And what did he do?

CODY: Leave it alone, alright?

SISTER: The man who was with you. What was he doing? *(Silence)* Come on, Cody?

CODY: *(In a whisper)* What?

SISTER: What did he do once you were High?

CODY: He. Umm. Stayed.

SISTER: And?

CODY: What?

(Pause)

SISTER: Did you tell anyone?

CODY: Not really.

SISTER: Why not?

CODY: Cause it kept happening. He would come to the trailer. Get my mom tweaked out. Then come after me while she was fucked up. It got to where I would just shoot up every time I saw his truck pulling up. I mean. I knew what was going to happen. I might as well make it easier on myself, right?

SISTER: How many times did this—

CODY: I dunno. A lot. I don't remember.

SISTER: You said "not really".

CODY: Huh?

SISTER: When I asked if you had told anyone. You said "not really". What did you mean?

CODY: My mom found out.

SISTER: So you did tell her?

CODY: No. She saw him. One night. On top of me.

SISTER: What did she do?

CODY: She threw my ass out.

SISTER: She saw him raping you and she threw *you* out?

CODY: That's not what she saw. She just saw me lying there. Ya know? Like a faggot. That's what she called me anyway. A faggot. Then threw me and my stuff outside.

SISTER: Where did you go?

CODY: With him.

SISTER: Who him?

CODY: That guy.

SISTER: Why on earth would you--??

CODY: (*Exploding*) I WAS THIRTEEN YEARS OLD! WHAT THE FUCK ELSE WAS I GONNA DO??!

SISTER: Alright. Alright. Cody. I'm sorry. I had no right to... I'm. (*Beat*) So you—what? Moved in with him?

CODY: Yeah. And we started making money together.

SISTER: How?

CODY: Jesus Christ! How do you think? He would break me off a cut of whatever I made. Not much, but enough to get the hell out of there. Then I started hustlin' on my own and it felt real fuckin' good not to need nobody. But then the hustlin' led to drugs, and drugs to dealin', dealin', money, money, more drugs, more drugs, hustle but then it was all fucked up and

that's when I met... *(He stops mid-sentence.)* Can I go
now?

Scene 6

SISTER: What is it about the relationship between a
mother and son? Either there is too much love—or
none at all.
Take Saint Augustine's mother. Too much. Now her
son was a total fuckup. He was. Loved his whores and
liquor. His wild years lasted decades. And his Mama?
While Auggie was busy engaging in a life of great
sin—and I do mean doing dirty dirrrrty things—his
sainted Mother spent most of her time—*praying for him.*
So who was the real koo-koo magoo there, huh?
It was in the midst of all this insanity—Augustine
composed his most famous and controversial of
prayers: *Da mihi castitatem et continentiam, sed noli modo.*
"Grant me chastity and continence. But not yet!"
Oh, come on. I love that prayer. Look. We all ask God
for help. But only when it's convenient. Only when all
else fails do we seek His guidance.
Saint Augustine was no exception. He finally did turn
his life around—but only after a profound personal
crisis— Which, I'm sorry to say, is usually what it takes
for us to get our shit together.

Scene 7

(SISTER approaches FATHER.)

SISTER: Your sister did a fucking number on that kid.

(No response)

SISTER: Did you know she was a prostitute?

FATHER: Can we not get into this now?

SISTER: That Cody was continually raped by one of her regulars? That he was forced to have sex for money when other kids his age were still in grade school?

FATHER: So much for patient confidentiality.

SISTER: Why didn't you do anything to help him?

FATHER: Up until a few years ago I didn't even know he existed.

SISTER: How is that possible?

FATHER: We found out about Cody after my sister died.

SISTER: You must have gotten custody.

FATHER: My parents did. But he didn't want to live with them. And they sure as hell couldn't handle him. So it was—

SISTER: What?

FATHER: Complicated. Look. If I want to be in his life now? It has to be on his terms.

SISTER: Meaning he only calls when he needs something and when he doesn't—

FATHER: —I stay away.

SISTER: Text book behavior. Puts him in control.

FATHER: Right.

(Beat)

SISTER: Father. Cody needs far more intensive care than we have to offer. The drugs, the deliberate self harm, the anti-social maybe even *criminal* behavior needs to be addressed.

FATHER: Which is precisely why he's here and what you should be doing.

SISTER: You know we're not equipped to deal with this sort of thing. More importantly, *I'm* not equipped.

You have to call the State and get him into a more aggressive treatment program.

FATHER: Absolutely not. We have been given guardianship by the Court. If we imply we're incapable in any way that could prompt an investigation. We could lose our license. Not to mention the funding that accompanies a non-profit.

SISTER: So it's a matter of money?

FATHER: It's a matter of principle.

SISTER: Yours or mine?

FATHER: Just do your best with him.

SISTER: I don't know how.

FATHER: Find a way.

SISTER: No. If you're so hell-bent on keeping Cody here, assign him another counselor.

FATHER: It needs to be you.

SISTER: Father. I have been down this road before. And if we continue getting involved like this, Cody is going to hurt us in ways from which we may never recover. So. For him. For us. For me. Please. Release me from this.

(FATHER *starts to move off.*)

SISTER: *(Getting louder)* You know he's not finished. He doesn't want to get clean. His addiction is far too strong and he is unwilling to fight it.

FATHER: Will you keep your voice down?

SISTER: The only way he can possibly get sober is to have some major incident wake his ass up.

FATHER: He nearly died. Is that not incident enough?

SISTER: By his own *choosing*.

FATHER: No.

SISTER: That was no overdose.

FATHER: Sister.

SISTER: It was attempted suicide.

FATHER: We don't know that!

SISTER: What about the other one? The Boy who died.

FATHER: Why do you keep going back to that?

SISTER: Because Cody's hiding something. And until he gets honest about that—about everything—he is only going to do more damage to himself and everyone else who crosses his path.

(Pause)

FATHER: *(Slowly with great reverence)* "For what I do is not the good I want to do; no, the evil I do not want to do—but this I keep on doing." "There is a way that seems right to a man, but in the end it leads to death." "Do not conform to the evil desires you had when you lived in ignorance. For just as he who called you is holy—"

SISTER: "—so be holy in all you do." What do these random quotes have to do with anything?

FATHER: God always works through people, Sister. We witness that every day here. He will place someone in our lives at any given time so that a change in behavior can happen. Bring us to a better level of understanding. God has placed you now in Cody's path. All you need to do is remove the compulsion and replace it with something more meaningful. With faith. Because once you do that? He *will* have a spiritual awakening.

Scene 8

(An insistent knock is heard pounding.)

CODY: *(Offstage)* Sister?! Open up! Sister, are you in there?!!

SISTER: Cody? Is that you? What's—

CODY: Help me!

(A door is heard opening, then slams.)

SISTER: Oh, my God.

(CODY enters with a bloody right arm. A broken needle is sticking out as he stumbles inside followed by an increasingly frantic SISTER.)

SISTER: What have you done??

CODY: The needle went right through.

SISTER: My God. Cody. Why?

CODY: Take me to the hospital.

SISTER: No! You go there and they'll lock you up.

CODY: But.

SISTER: Stay right there. I mean it. Don't move. *(She runs offstage.)*

CODY: Hurry. It hurts.

SISTER: *(Offstage)* Of course it hurts, you stupid shit!

CODY: I thought you were going to stop swearing.

(SISTER returns with a first aid kit.)

SISTER: And I thought you were going to stop using.

CODY: I.

SISTER: Shut up and sit still. You button-holed the vein.

CODY: What's that mean?

(SISTER *takes a bottle of alcohol and pours it on* CODY's *arm. He screams in pain.*)

SISTER: I'm sorry. Did that sting?

CODY: Yeah!

SISTER: Good. (*She pours more alcohol on the arm.*)

CODY: You crazy bitch!

SISTER: You have no idea. (*She retrieves a pair of tweezers from the kit.*) Alright. This is going to hurt. A lot.

CODY: Great.

SISTER: Squeeze my arm.

CODY: I'm not a wimp. I can—

SISTER: Squeeze my fucking arm!!

CODY: Alright. (*He does so.*)

SISTER: Harder.

CODY: I don't want to hurt you.

SISTER: Try.

(CODY *squeezes harder.*)

SISTER: That a boy. Now: Deep breath. One. Two.

(CODY *screams as* SISTER *pulls the remaining needle from his arm. She takes some gauze from the first aid kit and begins wrapping.*)

SISTER: What was in the syringe?

CODY: Crank.

SISTER: Meth?

CODY: Yeah.

SISTER: Alright. I've got to apply some pressure. It might push the meth into the vein. And you could get a little High. So if I were you—I'd enjoy it while you can.

(SISTER *applies pressure with the gauze in an effort to stop the bleeding.* CODY *instantly coughs.*)

SISTER: Cody?

(CODY *continues coughing. Then no response.*)

SISTER: You alright?

(CODY *immediately feels the effects of the drug.*)

CODY: *(Tripping)* I'm High, Sister.

SISTER: You need to lie down.

(CODY *takes off his tank-top.*)

SISTER: What are you doing?

CODY: I'm going to have a little fun.

SISTER: Cody.

CODY: You remember fun. Don't you, Sister? (*He unzips his pants, they fall to the floor. He is completely naked, approaches her.*)

SISTER: Put your clothes back on.

CODY: Why? You turned on?

SISTER: I'm calling Father Michael.

(SISTER *starts off but* CODY *stops her, grabbing her from behind so she can't escape.*)

CODY: *(Seductively in a whisper)* You remember this. That feeling. That rush. What it does to you. Your body. Your mind. Tingling. Needing. Wanting.

(SISTER *tries to pull away.*)

CODY: You think you're so damn better than me. Cause you stopped. Cause you got clean. Cause you found God. But that's all crap. Cause I know the truth.

SISTER: And what would that be?

CODY: That you miss this. That you think about getting High every day. So you can feel what I'm feeling right now. (*He touches her inappropriately.*)

SISTER: Knock it off!

CODY: Or what?

(*Silence*)

CODY: You talk a tough game, Sister. Put on this big front. But you're fucking scared right now. Aren't you? Of what I'm going to do to you. What I could do.

(SISTER *releases herself, throws* CODY *to the floor.*)

SISTER: You little shit. You think you have power over me? I've fought bigger monsters than you my whole life. Come on, Cody. Try.

(CODY *doesn't move.*)

SISTER: Show me what it's like to be with a real man. Oh. Wait. I forgot. You're not attracted to women. Only little boys.

CODY: Shut up!

SISTER: And why is that I wonder. Because they can't fight back?! (*She slaps him hard across the face. Long pause. Breathless*) There's. Umm. A blanket. In the closet. I'll go and—You'll sleep here tonight. Don't wander outside. Or back to your room. If anyone sees you like this you'll wind up in jail. (*She starts off.*) Oh, and Cody? (*She turns back.*) You ever pull this shit with me again? I'll beat the fuck out of you. I will. And I won't think twice about it.

Scene 9

(FATHER is saying a Rosary.)

FATHER: Hail Mary, full of grace.
Our Lord is with thee.
Blessed art thou among women,
and blessed is the fruit of thy womb, Jesus.
Holy Mary, Mother of God,
pray for us sinners now
and at the hour of our death. Amen.

(CODY has fallen asleep. SISTER enters with a blanket and covers his naked body.)

FATHER: Hail Mary, full of grace.
Our Lord is with thee.
Blessed art thou among women,
and blessed is the fruit of thy womb, Jesus.
Holy Mary, Mother of God,
pray for us sinners now
and at the hour of our death. Amen.

(SISTER retrieves her Rosary beads and begins praying in unison with FATHER.)

FATHER & SISTER: Hail Mary, full of grace.
Our Lord is with thee.
Blessed art thou among women,
and blessed is the fruit of thy womb, Jesus.
Holy Mary, Mother of God,
pray for us sinners now
and at the hour of our death.

(Three beats)

FATHER & SISTER: Amen.

(Blackout)

END OF ACT ONE

ACT TWO

Scene 1

SISTER: On Sunday mornings my parents would take Teresa to the 8 A M Mass. I usually slept in, due to my late hours the night before—for which I was always punished. But attendance at church was mandatory. So I would be sent off to the 11 A M Mass with strict orders to come directly home afterwards.

Each week my father would give me two quarters. One to place in the basket at the Offertory and the other after Communion in the second collection. And that's exactly what I did—for two weeks.

But one Sunday as I was walking to Church, the Devil himself decided to walk with me. *(With an Irish accent)* "You know, Jamie,"—he said. (The Devil is Irish) —"if you were to leave church early and skip Communion, you could take that second quarter to buy yourself an ice cream soda down at the bowling alley, flirt with that boy you like so much and still be home by 12:15." Well, let me say this about the Devil: he is never without options.

So for months that's exactly what happened. And it all worked out perfectly—until the dreaded Christmas Pageant of 1969. Teresa was playing Mary. Of course. I was a sheep or some kind of fucking cattle-- I don't know. Anyway. We're all walking back to the car when suddenly Monsignor Cabrera makes a bee line right for me.

And in front of my entire family, he asks why I always leave Church every Sunday before receiving Communion. Well. What could I do—but lie to his face. "Oh no, Monsignor. You must be mistaken". He asks again. I lie some more. "No. Monsignor, you must be mistaking me for someone else". He asks one last time. Well now I am outraged. "Monsignor, do I look like the kind of girl who would lie to a man of God?" Thankfully, the cock did not crow that night. Monsignor apologized, wished me a very Merry Christmas and actually believed me. My parents, on the other hand, knew me for the filthy liar I was, gave all my presents that year to the local children's hospital and stripped me of any remaining privilege I had left as a human being.

Temptation. When you give into it? It never ends well.

Scene 2

(SISTER *approaches a sleeping* CODY, *looks at him. She walks over to the door and slams it. He is immediately startled.*)

SISTER: Oh, I'm sorry. Did I wake you?

CODY: (*Still groggy*) Good morning to you too.

SISTER: It's afternoon.

CODY: Do you always have to correct me?

SISTER: Do you always have to be wrong?

(*Beat*)

CODY: So.

SISTER: What?

CODY: How are you?

SISTER: Don't make small-talk with me.

CODY: What are you going to do?

SISTER: Call Father Michael. Tell him you've relapsed.

CODY: Why do you gotta do that?

SISTER: Because you don't deserve my help.

CODY: Look. I screwed up. Alright? I'm sorry.

SISTER: Save it. You're boring me.

CODY: Look, if anyone finds out about this—

SISTER: —you go to jail. Yes. I'm well aware of that fact.

CODY: And won't you feel bad if I do?

(Beat)

SISTER: *(Then softening)* Do you even *believe* in God?

CODY: No.

SISTER: Why not?

CODY: Look at the life He's given me.

SISTER: Ahhh. Then you *do* believe. You think God has done this to you.

CODY: Whatever.

SISTER: That's not God, Cody. That's people.

CODY: I don't care, alright?

SISTER: People disappoint. God never does.

CODY: Whatever.

SISTER: God loves you.

CODY: Call Father Michael already.

SISTER: He wants you to be happy and free of this addiction.

CODY: Call him!

(SISTER takes a rosary from her pocket, puts it in CODY's hands.)

SISTER: Here.

CODY: What is this?

SISTER: We're going to pray.

CODY: Fuck that.

SISTER: We're going to say a Rosary together.

CODY: No way.

SISTER: And when we finish? What happened last night will be forgotten and unspoken.

(Beat)

CODY: You mean you won't tell?

SISTER: *(Agreeing)* Forgotten and unspoken.

CODY: I don't even know what a Rosary is.

SISTER: I'm going to teach you. *(She gives him a small prayer book.)* Take the Crucifix in your hand.

(CODY *does so.*)

SISTER: Now. Make the sign of the Cross. *(She takes his hand in hers and makes the sign of the cross on his body.)* In the name of the Father, and of the Son and of the Holy Spirit…

CODY: You swear you won't tell?

SISTER: Read.

(CODY *attempts to read from the prayer book.*)

CODY: I. B. B. Bel.

SISTER: *(Realizing)* —believe.

CODY: Believe. In. G. God. Th. The. Fa. Fa.

SISTER: Father.

CODY: Father. Al. All. Alm. Alm— *(In frustration, he throws the book down, fighting back tears. Pause)*

SISTER: *(Softly/Motherly)* Cody. It's alright. It's okay. We'll. Umm. We'll just try this another way. Alright?

(CODY *nods.*)

SISTER: Just repeat what I say:
I believe in God. The Father Almighty. Creator of heaven and earth. I believe in Jesus Christ. His only Son. Our Lord.

CODY: I believe in God. The Father Almighty. Creator of heaven and earth. I believe in Jesus Christ. His only Son. Our Lord.

SISTER: Don't look down. There's no shame in this.

(CODY *raises his head, looks up at* SISTER.)

SISTER: I believe in the Holy Spirit. The communion of Saints. The forgiveness of sins. The resurrection of the body and life everlasting. Amen.

CODY: I believe in the Holy Spirit. The communion of Saints. The forgiveness of sins. The resurrection of the body and life everlasting. Amen.

SISTER: Now take the first bead.

(CODY *does so.*)

SISTER: Our Father, who art in heaven,

CODY: Our Father, who art in heaven,

Scene 3

(In prayer)

SISTER: Okay God, here's the deal: I know we have had somewhat of a tumultuous relationship. There was a long period when I didn't believe You existed. When I

felt abandoned. And I know I'm not perfect. I'm hardly
like the others who serve You. I'll be the first to admit
sometimes my faults far outweigh my abilities. But
that's just me. I am trying to do Your work here. And.
Well. Lately. I'm finding I need help.

This kid's had one shitty life. And I'm not blaming
You for that. It is what it is. I get that. I do. But none
of this is his fault. From the day he was born he never
had a chance. So why does he have to suffer like this?
(Beat) I think it's time we give him a break. And I'm not
getting lazy. I'll do my part. I'll work my ass off to help
him. But you need to meet me half way. Or else this
just isn't going to work.

You know I don't believe you can receive the miracle
of healing without *asking* for it. Without *wanting* it. But
just this once—how about I ask for him? How about
that?

Lord Jesus I ask that You bring this child peace. Mary,
blessed Mother of God, help free your son Cody from
the bondage of self. And Holy Spirit, let your Light
perpetually shine upon him. And finally—please—
grant him—*serenity.*

Scene 4

(Back with CODY*)*

CODY: In the name of the Father and of the Son and of
the Holy Spirit. Amen.

SISTER: See? You're starting to remember it. How did
that feel?

CODY: Stupid.

SISTER: Good. That means you're doing it right.

(Beat)

CODY: I'm never going to beat this thing.

SISTER: Why do you say that?

CODY: Look what I keep doing to myself. After all the shit that's gone down. I just keep going back for more.

SISTER: That's our disease, kiddo.

CODY: I don't buy that.

SISTER: Why else would someone do the same thing over and over—completely knowing the horror that awaits them—risking their life time and time again? Why?

(CODY *remains silent.*)

SISTER: Did I ever tell you the story about the Frog and the Scorpion?

CODY: No and please don't.

SISTER: So there's this scorpion who wanted to cross a river. But scorpions can't swim.

CODY: *(Mumbling)* Arrgh.

SISTER: So he sees this frog sitting next to him on a river bank. And he asks the frog if he could climb up on his back so the frog could carry him across the water. But the frog, he's not too cool with this idea. How does he know the scorpion won't just kill him. Right? But the scorpion poo-poos that and says "Why no. For if I were to do that, we would both surly die." Because as we all know—scorpions can't swim. Are you with me?

CODY: Does it matter?

SISTER: No. So. The scorpion climbs upon the frog's back who starts to swim across the river. But half way there, he suddenly feels a sharp piercing in his back and out of the corner of his eye he sees the scorpion withdraw his stinger. As his limbs slowly grow numb and his body becomes paralyzed the frog cries out, "You fool! Why would you do such a thing? Now we shall both surely die! Why did you do this?" Well the scorpion just shrugs as they slowly sink into the water. "I cannot help myself. It is my nature. Self destruction. It is my nature." Glug-glug. Glug-glug-glug. Glug-Glug.

CODY: That was a total downer.

SISTER: That is what's going to happen to us if we don't change our nature. Last week. When you went out and used. What brought that on?

CODY: I don't know.

SISTER: Bullshit.

CODY: I *don't*. I just. I dunno. I've just been thinking about stuff lately.

SISTER: Like what?

CODY: What I told you.

SISTER: About your mother and—

CODY: —what happened to me and how I fucked up my life.

SISTER: Alright. Good. So your past is your trigger.

CODY: What do you mean "trigger"?

SISTER: Your reason for getting High. Cody, all these years you've had to live with such shame. The shame of being an unwanted child. The shame of watching your mother give herself to strangers. The shame of selling the one precious thing that God gave you. And when something triggers our shame? We shift into avoidance mode. And how do we avoid?

CODY: I dunno.

SISTER: Yes you do.

CODY: By drinking and doing drugs.

SISTER: Bingo. So. In walks your old friend Shame. What did you do? Come on. Talk me through it.

CODY: I bolted outta here. Called someone I knew would have some stuff. And I met him.

SISTER: Keep going.

CODY: He gave me some crank. I gave him—*you know*—and then I split.

SISTER: And was there ever a moment in the midst of this insanity– even a split second when you thought about *not* doing it. That you thought of the crash afterwards or what trouble you might get into or, or, or me even. Cody. Did you think even once about me?

CODY: Sure. I thought about you a couple times.

SISTER: Then why didn't you call? Or come talk to me?

CODY: I didn't think I could.

SISTER: You can. No. You *must*. If you want any chance of getting clean. (*Beat*) But you don't want that. Do you?

(*An uncomfortable silence passes between* CODY *and* SISTER.)

CODY: Look. I know what you've been trying to do. What you want me to become and shit. And I think it's really awesome of you to try. But I can't be that for you. I don't belong here.

SISTER: Then what *are* you doing here?

CODY: I don't know. Ever since Father Michael found me all fucked up in my motel room that night—

SISTER: Wait. Wait. *Father Michael* found you? He told me it was the police.

CODY: Who do you think called them?

Scene 5

(SISTER *approaches* FATHER.)

SISTER: You were there.

FATHER: Hmm?

SISTER: In the motel room.

FATHER: What are you talking about?

SISTER: Cody told me you were the one who found him that night.

FATHER: He was barely conscious. How can he possibly remember any details of that night?

SISTER: He seemed pretty clear to me.

FATHER: Well. He's mistaken.

SISTER: I don't think he is.

FATHER: And I don't have to justify myself to—

SISTER: (*Overlapping/insistent*) What were you doing in that motel room?

(*Beat*)

FATHER: I spoke to Cody earlier that day. But he was acting—different than usual. Despondent.

SISTER: So you *did* know he was thinking about killing himself.

FATHER: Yes. I went to check in on him and when he didn't answer the door I panicked. Told the woman at the front desk my concerns. So she opened his room and I found him there.

SISTER: You mean *them*. You found *them* there.

FATHER: The boy was already dead. But Cody was still conscious. So I called for an ambulance and he was admitted into the hospital.

SISTER: What happened with the police?

FATHER: Does it really matter?

SISTER: Yes.

(Beat)

FATHER: I flushed the drugs and paraphernalia down the toilet and got rid of any money before they arrived.

SISTER: Why would you put yourself in that position?

FATHER: So they couldn't arrest Cody for dealing.

SISTER: Then why was he charged with possession?

FATHER: I guess I missed some things. There wasn't a lot of time and I wasn't in my right head. So. I convinced the Court to let him do a twenty-eight day program here instead of any jail time.

SISTER: *(Under her breath)* Amazing.

FATHER: Which was the best thing for him. I mean, you see how he's getting better.

SISTER: Oh, you are fooling yourself.

FATHER: No. Cody promised. He promised me that this time he's really going to—

SISTER: HE RELAPSED!

FATHER: What?

SISTER: About a week ago. Snuck out, turned a trick and used the money to buy drugs.

FATHER: Why did you let him leave?

SISTER: As if I could really stop him.

FATHER: Is he alright?

SISTER: No! Father. This is what I have been trying to tell you. We are not helping him by keeping him here!

FATHER: I won't send him anywhere else!

SISTER: Why not?!

FATHER: BECAUSE I FINALLY HAVE HIM HERE
WITH ME! *(Pause)* She tried to contact me. My sister
tried to contact me. A week or so before she died. I
hadn't heard from her in years. So I don't know why
she was—maybe just reaching out or wanted to talk to
someone. I don't know. *(Beat)* I never called her back.
Never told my parents. I mean, to bring all that back
up again—to relive all that—I didn't know what to do
back then. But I do now. And I'm not going to make
that same mistake with Cody.

SISTER: How long have you been enabling him?

FATHER: I have been trying to help Cody.

SISTER: I know that's what it seems like to you. But this
may be a factor in why he can't get clean.

FATHER: Because of me?

SISTER: Your interference is keeping him from hitting
his bottom. Maybe he should go to jail.

FATHER: No. He has to be with me. He has to stay with
me.

SISTER: I need to know what you've been doing.
Specifically.

(No answer)

SISTER: Michael, please?

FATHER: So I give him money sometimes.

SISTER: Which he spends on drugs.

FATHER: Set him up in a place to live every now and
then.

SISTER: Which he trashes and gets evicted from.

FATHER: I buy him clothes. Groceries.

SISTER: Jesus.

FATHER: I won't abandon him.

SISTER: You have to stop doing this.

FATHER: I'm all that kid has.

SISTER: And apparently his fallback. Why the hell should he stop using if you're always right there to pick up the pieces??

FATHER: You didn't seem to be complaining when I did that for you. Last year, after that car accident. Which was it now, Sister? A, a tree? Telephone pole? Oh wait. You don't remember. You were drunk.

SISTER: It was a slip.

FATHER: That's a pretty word for an ugly situation.

SISTER: A moment of weakness.

FATHER: And an incident I alone helped to diffuse.

SISTER: You know how difficult that case was for me.

FATHER: And you know you would be gone right now if it wasn't for me.

SISTER: People make mistakes.

FATHER: That's right. We do.

Scene 6

SISTER: The next right step.
In Catechism we are taught that the only way to grow closer to God is to take—the next right step. But. Where our teachers fail to instruct us is in what that next right step might *be*.
Now. Some say it is the conscience. That little voice within us that guides us in the right direction. The problem with that is there's this *other* voice. *Not* the conscience. The Survivor. And the Survivor wants us to do whatever it takes to protect itself.

So. We have truth. And we have lie. Many times in life
a truth must be withheld and a lie will ultimately be
told. Because it's never just one or the other. No. Our
lives are a perfect blend of truth *and* lie. And we all do
it. And we all deny it. And we all judge one another for
doing the exact same thing.
Sometimes the Conscience wins. Sometimes the
Survivor.
The next right step.

Scene 7

(CODY, FATHER, *and* SISTER *are together for the first and
only time.*)

SISTER: I'm not doing this anymore. The lying. The
covering up.

FATHER: Sister. I would like a word with you in private.

SISTER: No. No more secrets. Cody, I'm sorry but I have
not been helping you.

CODY: What do you mean?

SISTER: We all know there's been a violation here. And
it must be reported.

FATHER: You don't have the authority to do that. It has
to go through me.

SISTER: (*To* FATHER) I did go through you. But you
don't have the balls to do anything about it! (*To* CODY)
Cody, it's time you start taking responsibility for your
actions.

CODY: You told me you were cool with this.

SISTER: Well, I'm not.

CODY: Then what was all that "forgotten and
unspoken" bullshit??

FATHER: Would you stop upsetting him?

SISTER: When you start standing up to him.

CODY: What is going on?!

FATHER: She's talking about your relapse.

CODY: You told him??

FATHER: She did. And it's okay.

CODY: You lied to me?

SISTER: Yes. And I'd be lying if I don't report it.

CODY: But you promised!

SISTER: Cody, I cannot stand by and watch you self-destruct.

CODY: So what? You're kicking me outta here now?

FATHER: No. Buddy. You're not in trouble.

SISTER: Yes he is.

FATHER: You're overstepping your bounds.

SISTER: You put me in charge of this kid and I'm going to do whatever it takes to get him clean. Even if that means going to the Archdiocese.

FATHER: They won't listen to you.

SISTER: They will if I tell them this patient is your nephew.

CODY: I thought you said we weren't gonna say nothin' about that.

FATHER: It's alright. There's nothing you need to worry about.

SISTER: There is if I report Cody left the premises and used.

CODY: You wouldn't do that.

FATHER: Sister, they will throw him in jail.

SISTER: That's right. They will. But you are going to convince them of an alternate sentence.

FATHER: Which is what?

SISTER: Six months. Maximum security rehab.

CODY: *(Begging)* No. Uncle Mike. Please don't let her do this to me.

FATHER: Buddy, she's not going to do anything. I promise.

CODY: I'll get clean. I swear.

FATHER: I know you will.

SISTER: That's his disease talking.

CODY: I just need more time.

FATHER: Okay. You got it. No worries.

SISTER: It's trying to bargain with you.

CODY: Fuck you!

SISTER: Father, listen to me. Our only hope is to send him away. To force him to stop hurting himself.

FATHER: And what if I say no?

SISTER: Then you are sicker than he is.

(Beat)

FATHER: I. I. I can't.

SISTER: I'm going to report this. *(She starts off.)*

CODY: Uncle Mike!

(FATHER darts in front of SISTER.)

FATHER: Look. He made a mistake. He won't do it again.

SISTER: Are you listening to yourself?

FATHER: Can't we just forget about it?

SISTER: If this were any other patient—

FATHER: Cody is not any other patient.

SISTER: He's the same addict with the same behavior. And you need to get the fuck out of his way!

CODY: Uncle Mike, you're not believing this shit, are you?

FATHER: I.

CODY: Look. I'll do whatever you want.

FATHER: Buddy.

CODY: I'll go to meetings. I'll get a job. I'm getting clean.

SISTER: He's lying to you.

CODY: Shut up.

SISTER: Like he's done every time before.

CODY: Uncle Mike. Please.

SISTER: His addiction is trying to stay alive.

CODY: It'll be different this time.

SISTER: No it won't.

CODY: (To SISTER, crazed) WHY ARE YOU DOING THIS TO ME?!

SISTER: Look at him. His disease has consumed him. He needs to take one contrary action. Do something he doesn't want to do.
Father. For the love of God. Help this child by putting him away.

(Long pause)

FATHER: (To Sister) Alright. Alright.

CODY: No. No fuckin' way. You ain't lockin' me up for no six fucking months.

FATHER: Cody.

CODY: *(To Father Michael)* You fucked over my mother and you ain't gonna to do it to me. Fuck you! I don't need this shit! FUCK BOTH OF YOU!

(CODY exits. FATHER instinctively bolts toward the door.)

SISTER: Don't you dare!

FATHER: But I need to —

SISTER: One. Contrary. Action. *(Beat)* Look. Obviously neither one us is any good at playing God. We have to be still. Hope we are doing the right thing.

FATHER: Will you do me one favor?

SISTER: If I can.

FATHER: Go find him.

SISTER: No, that's not a good idea-

FATHER: Please. I need to know that he's safe. Once we get him back here I swear I will do things your way.

SISTER: Sounds like you have more faith in me than in God.

FATHER: God doesn't need to save Cody, you do. *(He exits.)*

Scene 8

SISTER: *(With increasing difficulty)* I often try to forget his name. That boy from the bowling alley. I invited him back to the house one night after his shift. My parents were gone for the weekend. Enticing him with the key to Daddy's liquor cabinet and the possibility of getting lucky.
We drank and got high down in our rec room while Teresa was sleeping upstairs. I must have gotten completely wasted or maybe he slipped something in my drink because—well—I don't know. I passed

out. Or something. I don't—(*Beat*) When I woke up a few hours later? He was gone. I looked everywhere for him. I dragged myself upstairs. Body weak. Vision blurred.

As I reached the top landing, I saw the light under Teresa's door. I knocked but—no answer. So I went in. The first thing I saw was her torn nightgown on the floor. Ripped panties at the bottom of the bed. She was lying there. Naked. Motionless. She was raped. Strangled. Dead. He must have gone up there to be with her. Instead of staying downstairs. With me.

My parents blamed me of course. For not watching over her. For bringing a stranger in the house. For the drinking and the drugging and well—just—for all the—*shame*.

They locked him up for thirty-two years. And then he was released. He's probably out there somewhere— still doing what is his—*nature*.

I need to believe that people can and do change. That miracles happen to the most destitute of souls. And that God does forgive and offer salvation beyond the scientific data that guarantees only a third of us will survive—

See? Getting sober has always been the easy part for me. It's *staying* sober—that I just can't seem to— (*Her voice trails off.*)

(CODY *enters from the other side of the stage with a dirty syringe in his mouth. He takes off his shoelace and ties it around his arm. He attempts to find a vein but to no avail, hurting himself and wincing in the process. He takes off his shoe and sock, ties the shoelace around his ankle and finds a vein in his foot. He shoots up. Coughs. Euphoria*)

Scene 9

(SISTER *approaches* CODY.)

SISTER: Cody.

CODY: What are you doing here?

SISTER: I'm looking to buy a hustler.

CODY: Get bent.

SISTER: I'm serious. How much?

CODY: Depends on how long you want?

SISTER: Long enough to get through to you.

CODY: I'm not talking to you. You're a liar.

SISTER: I fucked up. I'm sorry. But sometimes we need to lie to those we care about to help them.

CODY: I'm a lost cause, Sister.

SISTER: No one is lost who has faith.

CODY: Can we not do this?

SISTER: Cody. I think I know a way to help you. There's a Sacrament called Reconciliation. It will allow you to confess your sins and in doing so you will be given a newfound freedom and be forgiven.

CODY: That won't help me.

SISTER: How do you know if you don't try?

CODY: Why can't you just leave me alone?

SISTER: Because I don't think that's what you really want. But if it is. Alright. You do this for me. You confess your sins to God and I will stay the hell away from you from now on.

CODY: What?

SISTER: Tell God you are heartily sorry for your sins and sorry that you have offended Him.

CODY: I'm sorry—

SISTER: No. Say His name.

CODY: God. I'm sorry. For sinning and offending You.

SISTER: Tell Him you are firmly resolved to confess your sins and do penance and amend your life.

CODY: I confess my sins and will do penance and amend my life.

SISTER: Tell God everything. Unload it all on me. Right here.

Start with your mother.

CODY: I. I hated her. I'm glad she's dead.

SISTER: What about the man?

CODY: I hate him too. I hate him for—

SISTER: Say it.

CODY: I hate the man who raped me.

SISTER: Did you ever retaliate?

CODY: I stole his car. His watch. His money.

SISTER: And other people?

CODY: I lied to them. Took stuff from them. Hurt them.

SISTER: Physically?

CODY: Sometimes. I would beat people up when they didn't do what I wanted.

SISTER: And sexually? Did you abuse anyone?

CODY: Lots of times. I fucked guys for drugs. Got fucked for money. I did that shit most of my life.

SISTER: What else?

CODY: That's it.

SISTER: You left out the Boy.

CODY: Leave me alone.

SISTER: There was a suitcase in the police report. It was packed with the Boy's clothing. Where was he going?

CODY: Nowhere.

SISTER: Tell God the truth so He can help you.

CODY: I don't need His help.

SISTER: You don't want to live like this.

CODY: I do.

SISTER: You never have to go back to this life again.

CODY: You don't get it.

SISTER: Tell Him, Cody.

CODY: No.

SISTER: What were you doing with the Boy?

CODY: I loved him.

SISTER: How?

CODY: I took care of him.

SISTER: How did you take care of him?

CODY: By making him do things.

SISTER: What things?

CODY: With men.

SISTER: Why?

CODY: We needed money.

SISTER: He was fourteen.

CODY: No more.

SISTER: No. You go on.

CODY: I can't trust you.

SISTER: You can.

CODY: You'll tell people.

SISTER: I won't.

CODY: You'll tell.

SISTER: Believe in Him.

CODY: Swear to God you won't tell.

SISTER: Allow the miracle.

CODY: Swear.

SISTER: Let God help you!

CODY: TELL ME YOU SWEAR TO GOD!

SISTER: I SWEAR TO GOD!

CODY: THEN I KILLED HIM!! *(Pause)* His parents found out what we were doing together. So they sent him a ticket. Just him. I asked him not to go. I begged him. To stay with me. But he said no.

SISTER: And that hurt you.

CODY: Real bad.

SISTER: Because people don't stay.

CODY: I went out. Scored some stuff. Some heavy stuff. I asked him if he wanted to get High with me one last time. He said no. But then he changed his mind. So I crushed it. Filled up the syringe. Shot him up. And then. I waited. With my arms around him. I waited. Until he was gone. Then I did myself. *(Breaking)* I thought there was enough left. But there wasn't. It didn't work. Cause I'm still here. And I don't want to be. I'm still here. I'm still—

(CODY lets out an uncontrollable sob as SISTER pulls away, leaving him alone in his sorrow. As she exits, he reaches for the Rosary beads around his neck and begins praying.)

CODY: Our Father, who art in heaven, hallowed be the name…

Scene 10

(An inebriated SISTER *approaches* FATHER.*)*

FATHER: It's almost dawn. Where were you last night?

SISTER: I. I was walking.

FATHER: Walking.

SISTER: Lost track of time I guess.

FATHER: Did you find Cody?

(No answer)

FATHER: Sister?

(Beat)

SISTER: They never told Her.

FATHER: Who?

SISTER: The Virgin Mother. They never told Her the truth.

FATHER: What are you babbling about?

SISTER: "Fear not, for thou hast found favor with the Lord."

FATHER: You need to sit down.

SISTER: But the angel never told Her the whole story. No one did.

FATHER: Will you please just—

SISTER: They knew what was going to happen but they kept it from Her. And there was nothing she could do but watch Her Child be tortured and suffer and—

FATHER: Would you stop already?!

(Pause)

SISTER: You want to know what I did last night, Father? You want to hear my big game plan? *I had Cody confess his sins to God.* But wait. That's not the crazy part. No.

The crazy part is that when he finally did—*I couldn't handle it.* I just—I walked away.

FATHER: What about forgiveness?

SISTER: Cody murdered that Boy. Do you really think God is going to forgive that?

FATHER: I'd like to think so. Wouldn't you?

SISTER: Father, what are we doing here?

FATHER: What do you mean?

SISTER: You and me. Why are we here?

FATHER: To help others. To serve God.

SISTER: No. That's what we tell everyone. What we try to convince ourselves of.

FATHER: Why stay here then?

SISTER: To hide. Because we still think it's safe. But eventually it's going to find us. No matter how tight we keep those windows shut or how many locks we put on those doors—it's going to find its way inside.

FATHER: What is?

SISTER: Our compulsions. *(She redirects.)* Cody must be hungry by now, I'll take him some food. Oh, and a coat. I don't remember if he had a coat. But I can bring him a change of clothes so he'll be—

FATHER: *(Overlapping)* He's dead. *(Beat)* Cody's dead. *(Pause)* The police just left. His body was found in some alley way.

SISTER: No. That's not true. I just saw him. That's not true!

FATHER: Overdose probably. Suicide maybe. Who knows. In any event. It's finished.

SISTER: I'm sorry.

FATHER: For what? My loss? That's what we're supposed to say, anyway. "I'm sorry for your loss." When my sister died. I stood by her casket for six hours as people would come up to me. And I'd have to listen to that same fucking line over and over. "I'm sorry for your loss". But what they really meant: "I'm glad I'm not you". *(Breaking)* Because once they were alone. Oh, I bet they would fall to their knees. Thanking God that it wasn't their younger sister whose body was found in a dumpster or their teenage nephew who laid dead on the street— *(Long pause)* You need to go.

SISTER: Where?

FATHER: The morning meeting.

SISTER: No. Father. No. I. I can't.

FATHER: You have patients waiting.

SISTER: You don't understand. Last night. After seeing Cody—

FATHER: I know. I know. Go get yourself together. *(He starts off.)*

SISTER: Father?

(FATHER turns back.)

SISTER: How can anyone live with this much pain?

FATHER: Some people have more faith. *(He exits.)*

Epilogue

(Children's laughter is heard again.)

SISTER: My sister and I used to take one another's hands. Twirling each other around and around. Spinning so fast and giggling so loud you could barely hear the words we were singing. And when we finally fell to the ground. We couldn't even lift our heads

from the grass. Because we would be so dizzy from
that rush. And every time we landed? That delightful
wooziness would become more and more terrifying.
But still we would do it over and over again. *(Singing)*
Ashes. Ashes. We all fall—
(Pause)
I decided to finally go back to Mass this morning. I
haven't been in weeks. So I thought I'd go. People start
getting suspicious when a nun stops going to Church.
Anyway. The second reading was from the Book of
Philippians. Where the apostle Paul talks about his
existence. He writes: "For to me, living means living
for Christ, and dying is even better. I am constantly
torn between these two desires."
That passage made me think of Cody. And that maybe
my prayers were answered. I don't know. Did a
miracle occur? Has Jesus brought him peace? Did Mary
help free him from himself? For the Boy is floating
far up into that sea of constellations. And has finally
found—*serenity.*
(Struggling) As for me? Well. I need to be up there. I
want—to be—*High.*

(Blackout)

END OF PLAY

www.ingramcontent.com/pod-product-compliance
Lightning Source LLC
Chambersburg PA
CBHW070026110426
42741CB00034B/2646